The Art of Living
Everything You Need
to Achieve Success in Life and Business,
I Learned in Prison

Daniel Simms

Cadmus Publishing
www.cadmuspublishing.com

Copyright © 2022 Daniel Simms
Published by Cadmus Publishing
www.cadmuspublishing.com
Port Angeles, WA

ISBN: 978-1-63751-078-0

All rights reserved. Copyright under Berne Copyright Convention, Universal Copyright Convention, and Pan-American Copyright Convention. No part of this book may be reproduced, stored in a retrieval system, or transmitted in any form, or by any means, electronic, mechanical, photocopying, recording or otherwise, without prior permission of the author.

Dedication

I would like to dedicate this book to all the people engaged in reversing the trend of America's reliance on mass incarceration. The first step is to understand the true cost to families, society, and individuals. 90% of inmates suffer from mental health and addiction. That's their true malady. Let us find a saner approach. If society provided treatment instead of incarceration it would destroy this insane return to prison in the first three years upon release. That is not solely due to the inmate. Society needs to bear some of that blame. And I am extremely thankful dialogue has begun on this dire topic.

Acknowledgments

First of all, I would like to thank my son Dillon. You are an inspiration son, the hardships you have been through already break my heart.

I love you forever son. I am the first to admit that my family is dysfunctional and fragmented. I wish that was not true. But it is. Regardless I still love them. Therefore, I would like to acknowledge my siblings David, Dennis, Douglas, and Kristine. I want them to know that despite their wanton neglect I am here for them.

Due to the state of my biological family, I have come to adopt others as my de facto family. First and foremost, I want to send my love to my foster father Mike Stanton, the owner of Seattle tree service. He lovingly accepted and cared for me when no one else did. Thank you. To my beautiful wife, Tracy Michelle Simms, for her invaluable help and support. To Benjamin Payne Ellis for his constant objectivity and creativity. To the Wright Family and in particular Michael Wright for their immeasurable positivity and contributions. To all those friends on social media that are helping get my voice out there. Acknowledgment goes out to all my incarcerated family I love you all.

Table of Contents

PROLOGUE 1
KEY ONE: You Can Be Your Own Worst Enemy or Your Own Best Champion. But, You Can't Be Both 7
KEY TWO: Get Over Yourself! To Truly Love and Enjoy Life You Need to Conquer Self-Importance 21
KEY THREE: Be Humble 27
KEY FOUR: Banish Vanity and Materialism 37
KEY FIVE: Quit Taking Yourself So Serious, Have Fun, Get Excited, And Think of Others 43
KEY SIX: Quit Making Excuses 49
KEY SEVEN: Solidify Your Dream into a Clearly Defined Goal 55
KEY EIGHT: Leap Into Action 61
KEY NINE: Ignorance is not bliss, Education is! 69
KEY TEN: Diligence and Hard Labor Leads to Happiness 77
KEY ELEVEN: Discern Fact from Fiction through Data And Learn from Mistakes 83
KEY TWELVE: Focus All Your Time, Energy, and Resources 91
KEY THIRTEEN: Be Original, Imaginative, and Innovative 97
ENCAPSULATION 102

PROLOGUE

Life is such an adventure! The moment we are counted out. Discounted by our families and friends. Left behind by prosperous acquaintances. And designated losers by society. That's when the human spirit, within each of us, can truly ascend to the greatest heights!

I feel so excited and honored to share this journey. To share the fundamental lessons I've learned that anyone can implement to achieve success. And I do not say "anyone" lightly. I truly mean anyone! No matter if you are in the depths of poverty. Addiction. Abuse. Or any other adverse afflictions. You can overcome your struggles. This is not a get-rich-quick methodology. It is a profound ideology that will change your life completely if you choose to follow it. The biggest thing I want to dispel immediately is that this book is all about me.

About my success. My journey. My answers for enlightenment. That's not what this is about. Not at all. I intended to create an artifice of empowerment. There are too many disparaging and negative influences in society today and I feel compelled to speak out! To call all people back to where they belong. That's where they were destined to be before society and outside influences stifled them.

Though the book is not meant as a self-aggrandizing autobiography, it will include considerable information about the first ideology that led me to success. I intend to use my platform to encourage the world to propel down the path that leads to fulfillment and happiness. If I can reach even one person then my goal will be complete. But my fantasy is that I'll reach thousands, millions, billions even. Transcending through generations. Reaching the hopeless ones, a hundred or success two hundred years from now. That would be amazing!

At points throughout the book, you may find sentences or thoughts that stand out to you. Please keep a highlighter or pen handy so you can underline it. Rereading and conjuring up important epiphanies will aid you in solidifying and crystallizing new thought processes. Life is all about learning. To effectively learn, one must definitively pursue understanding. To understand one must specifically dedicate their time, energy, and brainpower to the topic. I work best when I underline sentences. Write in the borders. And repeatedly meditate on whatever I'm pursuing. Keeping notes and physically writing them instead of typing them into a computer has been proven to increase retention considerably. I'm not implying that I'm an astute scholar that should be studied and quoted verbatim. That's the last thing I'd be saying! I'm just like you! A normal person! There's nothing special that I can do, that you can't also do! It's all about perspective. And that's what I'm trying to instill in you: a new perspective on life. A new perspective to revolutionize your future. And that's not all either, it can also revolutionize the lives of others around you.

In many aspects, I am merely sharing the truisms that I gathered from my years in the gutter. I learned the most through my hardships. Yes, it's true. We are strengthened by fire. Just like a soft ball of clay we all need to be shaped and tempered. It's that simple. If you are handed everything on a platter, you cannot grow and develop a true understanding of what it means to live life to the fullest. Television is chock full of shows that glamorize instant wealth, spoiled rich kids, or meaningless activities. But rarely does it highlight the real-world cost to achieve success. Sure, there are all kinds of game shows, singing contests, and reality shows that stoke flames of instant gratification. They all fall short of supplying a realistic path to success. Have you ever heard of the "Lottery Curse"? Well, it's the surprising assertion that a majority of large lottery winners end up experiencing emptiness and despairing effects. Why do you think this is? Is there truly a curse, or is there a better answer? I think there is a better answer. I believe what affected them was their perspective. They were so caught up in their windfall that they lost sight of themselves. They believed their happiness could be bought. They splurged and squandered their wealth on whatever caught their fancy. Thinking that was what they needed to obtain fulfillment. But then one day it probably hits them like a ton of bricks: I am hollow and unhappy. What they should've been doing instead of splurging was focusing on their internal development first. When you're not ready for something you can't effectively address it. That goes for anything. Wealth, fame, career advancement, children, and business ventures. Anything. First, we have to grow and develop the right frame of mind. The right perspective is critical. And that's what I seek to do, help you recognize how important it is to focus on yourself. Once you have implemented a positive forward-thinking ideology there is no limit to what your future could become.

One last note, I am coming from an abused and abandoned background, but the context in which I'm writing this is meant to appeal to everyone no matter their circumstances. Whether you are searching for something to help you overcome struggles or to pursue dreams this book can aid you. There is no quick fix for any problem but through continual growth, you can find what you're searching for. This volume is meant to supplement your ever-growing library of self-help and development books. You cannot achieve the unachievable unless you began to examine the arduous path to get there.

That's the beauty of life, everyone is so absorbed in obtaining instant gratification; true gratification, however, is only received from the journey. Hard work, diligence, education, experience, and persistence are the bricks paving the road to genuine success and fulfillment. Receiving something you work hard for, distills the appreciation that's required to truly enjoy it. So, let's shuck preconceived notions and all reservations to the wind and focus on making a better you!

THE ART OF LIVING

DANIEL SIMMS

THE ART OF LIVING

KEY ONE:

You Can Be Your Own Worst Enemy or Your Own Best Champion. But, You Can't Be Both

DANIEL SIMMS

THE ART OF LIVING

Guess what, I've got a newsflash for you. You are the key to your destiny. No one can determine your fate for you. Despite all the haters and detractors that would like you to believe otherwise. What you think, do, and pursue is completely your domain have you ever heard the word "sovereign" before? Most have heard it in the context of royalty or governments. But did you know, you are sovereign? Well, you are. You have sovereign will and authority over yourself. This means independent of anyone else you have the free ability to think and do whatever you want. Of course, lots of people, governments, and institutions would like you to be ignorant of this fact. If you don't know you can pull yourself out of poverty, then you will never try to. The same goes for any other circumstance, if you don't know or believe you can change it, you won't try to. And that is the crux facing people. They don't know how powerful their thoughts are.

The first step is to examine if you're a positive or negative person. This should be relatively simple. Do you wake up each morning with anticipation or trepidation? When you begin a project, do you feel excited or apprehensive? Do you look for all the reasons why it could go wrong? Why it could fail? How about when someone else embarks on a venture, do you disparage their efforts instead of supporting them? Don't be discouraged if you are a negative person. Overcoming the trait is only possible if you recognize you're susceptible to it. Denial only hurts you in the long run so it's best to come to grips with it now. Many people succumb to its influence. It stems from your unhappiness and lack of fulfillment. If you are happy and fulfilled, you will see the world in a whole new light. I promise that. So, as I said above, examine your personality, thought processes, and actions to see if you are negative or not. If you are not negative, you have dodged a major pitfall. Those that are inherently negative know exactly what I'm talking about. Unless you experienced the dark shadow of negativity, you cannot fully fathom its debilitating effects.

The good thing is, you can overcome negativity. It is only a thought process. Thought processes can be changed. It will take some work. But it can be done. You have to consciously make the effort to battle it. This is accomplished by refusing to dwell on anything negative. Only focus on the good. If you find yourself slipping backward, think of something that makes you happy. Something you have accomplished. Or something you did that made you feel good. You need to get into the practice of looking for the good in every circumstance, person, and venture. This is essential.

Quick succumbing to any temptation that leads you into doubting yourself, others, or particular outcomes. It is easier than you think to do. I say that because once you begin to consciously implement this philosophy your whole world will change. The change will manifest so quickly you'll be shocked. Instead of disparaging others, encourage them, you'll see immediately how it will impact them. Don't maintain a barrier of indifference and superficiality when you interact with others. You need to genuinely search for ways to support and encourage them instead. When you support others, they will support you.

You cannot stroll through life expecting to be included and encouraged by others unless first include and encourage them. I know some people might have others around them that are not exactly the positive type. I understand completely. That's why I say move on. It can be hard even to conceptualize moving on and away from family or friends that are negative but it's critical to your growth. This is not an epiphany that I arrived at lightly either. I had to implement it myself. Painfully. No one wants to be part of a negative environment. Not consumers. Employees. Or anyone else. So why would you intentionally want to be that way? Hopefully, you don't. If you currently have a negative personality then take some conscious efforts on changing it. No one can do it for you. It is dependent upon you. The way you look at the world, interact with it, and travel through it can be dramatically changed.

By consciously expanding effort to be upbeat, welcoming, inviting, and extremely friendly taught me a priceless lesson. Remaining positive on the inside will inherently exude to the outside. And that's why I strive every single day to be a beacon of light. Not only to friends and family but also to the prison guards. The hopeless inmates. Everyone. I want to exude positivity. Brightening everyone's day. Flashing heartfelt smiles to an overworked prison guard. Making sandwiches for the down on his luck hopeless inmate. I get pleasure from selflessly serving others in positive spirits.

I did, however, experience severe negativity for a time I did not always encounter positive influences. Matter of fact, the most important people in my life growing up, my parents, abandoned me on the steps of a foster home. I do not hold this against them. I love them immensely. But it was hard growing up in foster care. My mom was a deaf stay-at-home mother, and her love and dedication were readily apparent. But when she abandoned me, it was incredibly heartbreaking. She could not encourage me or support me. I desperately needed that from my mother. But she was unable to give it to me. For years I strived for approval. I tried everything. Cleaning around the house. Doing my schoolwork. Gardening. Listening and obeying her every command. I tried it all. But I could never make her happy. Since I was in my developmental years, I took her attitude personally. As if I was the cause of negativity. This caused me immense heartache. I yearned desperately for her affection but it never came. Whenever I accomplished something praiseworthy, she would quickly dismiss it or ignore it. But if I did one small mistake or blunder, she would pounce on it. It was like she searched diligently for my failures while refusing to acknowledge my successes. This hurt me. My mistakes were elevated and continually brought up to remind me of how much of a failure I was. I could never live them down. Being constantly reminded of my failures, while intentionally overlooking my successes, made me incredibly self-conscious. I thought I was a loser, pure and simple. For years I harbored feelings of defeat. I floated through my childhood, teens, and twenties nursing this mentality that was instilled by my mother. I did not try to speak out for fear of criticism. I did not try to excel in anything because I didn't believe I could. I withheld my praises towards others because I didn't feel they cared to hear them. I was a miserable person. A drag to be around.

It was hard to even look at myself in the mirror. And this detrimental thought process bled through to every aspect of my life, relationships, and choices. As you will find out in the chapters to come. Therefore, if anyone has the credibility to discuss overcoming negativity it's me. If I had not intentionally battled my flawed thought processes I'd still be in a cesspool of despair to this day. I would still be in a hopeless mind frame. Still cruising on a cloud of negativity and unhappiness. But I'm not. Not anymore!

I refused to continue down the avenue of hopelessness. I took the initiative. Grabbing my shoulders and shaking myself. How I looked at the world, people, and choices was my first obstacle. I challenged myself to find the good in everything. When I woke up, I immediately began the rigorous drills that changed me. Like a hairy caterpillar that starts the arduous process to become a beautiful butterfly, I transformed myself. I did this by telling myself, over and over, positive reinforcing statements. I am smart. I am a beautiful person inside and out. I am valuable. People want to hear my praises. People want me to speak out. I can do whatever I want to. If I put my mind to it, I can do anything. These are a few of my constant recitals. I needed to repeat them frequently throughout the day. Only with habitual recitation was I able to overcome mighty insecurities, negative thought processes, and hopelessness.

My whole life I have struggled with myself. I've always been extremely self-conscious. As millions of other people are. I tried to rein it in countless times. It never seemed to work. I'd set my mind to beginning a strict diet. Start a rigorous exercise routine. Or some other dietary fad. But they all lacked what I needed most: positive mental reinforcement. Therefore, I'd follow, dietary methodology for a while and the whole time I was unconsciously disparaging myself.

This diet isn't going to work. These exercises aren't helping. Why even try to change, it's useless. I can stand being negative.

But I can't stand working out every day. It's too hard. Too much work. And it's never going to increase my weightlifting abilities. I should just accept my body, as a fact of life that something that I can't change. My self-doubt and thought process prevented me from being successful in my weightlifting pursuits. At times I would reflect on recriminations my mother would sign to me. "You are not good enough". "You have issues". The words did not inspire me at all. Matter of fact, they did the opposite, they cause me to withdraw deeper inside myself. I found myself ignoring my issues completely. I refused to acknowledge them.

   I do not believe my mother said these things in spite. I think she generally thought the comments would propel me into bettering myself. I truly believe that. She had a negative personality, but she did love me, so the comments came from a good place. I like to believe. Despite her words, I have changed for the better. I am doing it! And it's because I took control of my thought process. I told myself I can do it. Every single day I recited and put it into action positively. The key to success. The key to insecurities. The key to negative thought processes. It is all entwined with your perspective. Pursue a positive perspective and you will obtain one! It's that simple. I am a testament to the power. If I can overcome so can you. As I was building myself up, I ran into an inordinate amount of negativity. Every time I turned around someone was detracting from my dream. "It's not going to work Daniel". "It is too big to take on". "People will continue to abandon you". "Why would people want to be friends with you?" "No one will accept this new Daniel; therefore, it must not be feasible". "You're wasting your time". "You are going to fail". The list of discouraging comments went on and on and on. And it did not stop either, it came when I shared my aspirations of a book too. "You aren't educated enough to write a book". "A high school diploma is not enough to adequately author anything, let alone a book". "No one wants to read a book about you". "You haven't even completed anything worthwhile yet and you're already writing a book! That's crazy!"

The criticism was intense. I was reaching too high. My aspirations were too lofty. People did not want to embrace them. They were so caught up on why it wouldn't work. Why it would fail. But not me. I was too caught up on why it was going to work. I saw all the good in it and none of the bad. My perspective chugged me through the storm of negativity like a train chugging through a category one tornado. As trees and debris of negativity crashed against my caboose my positive perspective repelled it. The negativity slid awkwardly like rain on dry seal skin.

I refused to allow anyone or anything to sway me. If I did, I knew my dreams would not be achieved. I cannot face that outcome. So, I buckled down and remain confident that everything would work out.

Some found my aspirations extremely audacious. Prisoner authors are sparse. But someone with my type of past and personality is extremely rare. There are none like me in the whole world. And I'm not talking about people that climbed out of abuse, foster care, and incarceration and became something special either. Although they should be proud of themselves too. I'm talking about taking an abstract book idea and seeing it to fruition. Seeing it become a book before my eyes. That takes grit. Tenacity. And confidence. All the things I lacked for years before I consciously pushed myself to have a positive perspective. Having a positive perspective is critical. You cannot do much without it. It's easy to stagnate in negativity because we are all creatures of habit. We all naturally want to stay within our particular comfort zones. But if you want to overcome the negative thought process you don't have that privilege. You have to consciously step into unfamiliar territory. It will be hard to change your perspective, but it can be done. Start small by reciting positive comments throughout the day to yourself. Then look diligently for people to praise. To complement. To help. It won't come naturally but keep working at it. Slowly but surely, you will be transformed. Will become the person people seek out for comfort. Your whole direction in life might change because of your new perspective. It will be extremely empowering to someday step back and look at how far you have gone. Life will have a purpose. Fulfillment. You will no longer be chained to negativity. What a blessing!

To me, perspective is encapsulated in every facet of human life. The way we perceive something dictates how we interact with it. For instance, in South America, there is a deeply impoverished city. The inhabitants subsist on very little. But this is not remarkable in itself. There are many impoverished cities in South America. This particular city, however, is different because it is built upon trash. All the surrounding cities dump their garbage receptacles such as aluminum, plastic, and various other materials to sell to recycling companies. The work is extremely dirty. Hard. Time intensive. And low paying. There is no doubt it's a grim existence. There is no guarantee they would gather enough to feed their children, let alone themselves. How could anyone, existing in this condition see anything but hardship and despair? Shouldn't they remain in a constant state of negativity? What would they have to be positive about? Right? Wrong!

You're not wrong that they don't have a lot of security or creature comforts to be positive about. But you are wrong that they all remained in a constant state of negativity. Some raised themselves above the environment. They refused to dwell on how bad the conditions were. Instead, they saw an opportunity. They have a positive perspective. When others saw garbage, they saw treasures. They saw what the garbage could be transformed into, not what it currently looks like.

This is perspective! And it's beautiful, isn't it? They took rusty pipes, nails, broken lamps, or other appliances and created musical instruments. Not just any musical instruments, they created every instrument that any renowned orchestra in the world would use to perform beautiful music. But they did not stop at creating musical instruments either. They also enlisted the children of the community to expand on that dream. They managed to teach these extremely impoverished children the rich value of musical harmony. And the result was pure ecstasy. They played exceptionally! When the world heard the gorgeous music emanating from the reclaimed garbage in the dumps of the South American city they were flabbergasted.

It awakens an incredible feeling of inspiration and pride in everyone that heard the Symphony. People wanted to hear of the unfortunate poverty-stricken individuals rising above their hardships. Pulling themselves above their struggles. Above their station in life as garbage pickers. To transform themselves into a world-class orchestra. Now musical theaters around the world are clamoring to book these remarkable expositions.

By changing their perspective on garbage. On their ability to learn and perform music. These individuals have effectively lifted themselves out of poverty, due completely to their perspective. How amazing is that! What can be changed in your life if you looked at it with new eyes? If you employed a new strategy. A new perspective. I would like to personally invite you to share them on our social media platforms I genuinely want to hear them.

I want to hear the excitement and discovery that emanates from your disclosures. When writing I always try to visualize the people I'm writing to as friends. This technique helped me immensely. The byproduct of this strategy is that I now consider you my friend. You took the time and energy to read my words which means there's a mutual effort between us. I expended effort to reach you through my writings. And you expended effort by consciously committing to reading this book and applying its concepts. Therefore, we are inextricably linked. Honestly, it makes writing a whole lot easier for me. I'm not writing for strangers. I'm writing to friends. Following that line of thought ensures I will truly value and appreciate any testimonials coming from every person that reads this book. Please take a moment and your thoughts and testimonies on any social media platforms. I will personally endeavor to read every posting.

THE ART OF LIVING

KEY TWO:

**Get Over Yourself!
To Truly Love and Enjoy Life You Need to Conquer Self-Importance**

DANIEL SIMMS

THE ART OF LIVING

I don't care if you are a multi-billionaire, the president of the United States, or an exceptional athlete of some sort, you still need to battle self-importance. Excessive pride, pompousness, arrogance, haughtiness, loftiness, and superiority are all forms of self-importance. And self-importance is not limited to those that have some measure of success. You can have excessive self-importance as a housewife. A fast-food employee. Or even as a homeless person. Excessive self-importance can touch every human being no matter who they are.

I would like to take a moment to add clarification. I know some individuals are questioning this practice of battling self-importance. They may be wondering how pride in their work, family, accomplishments, or possessions could possibly be wrong. Quite simply, it's not wrong. It only begins to become wrong when you indulge excessively in it. Everything in life should be done in moderation. Excessive eating leads to obesity. Excessive sun exposure leads to cancer. And excessive pride can lead to pompousness. Life is a gift. A true treasure. It should be experienced at peak level and that can only happen if you consciously overcome yourself.

Get over yourself.

I get it, you are special. You are a unique creature that has never been replicated in the past nor will be in the future. You have been endowed with certain inalienable attributes that can never be duplicated. You are extremely unique. Special. And precious. I cannot stress enough how incredible you are. Down to your DNA, fingerprints, and strands of hair. You are completely amazing! And that's just biology. Then there are your abilities. Wow! Humans can achieve such great heights with their awesome abilities! There is very little we cannot accomplish. When a problem, task, situation, or feat is discovered people began immediately to find the solution. This is unique to the human race. No other species has the ability that we have. That in itself is extraordinary! As a people, we should be extremely grateful for these qualities. Without them we would be climbing trees, sleeping in caves, and incapable of intelligent thought. We might have primal instincts, just like the other beasts of the field, but we would lack the ability to reach great heights as we can now.

There is no doubt, humans are exceptional beings. That is indisputable. Collectively we make great strides at advancing. And individually we can continue advancing our world each day.

Unfortunately, as great as humans are, we tend to let our ego and self-importance get the best of us. By allowing that to happen we stifle ourselves. When someone achieves a great feat it is extremely easy to allow that to define them. Whether you are educated, athletic, or have climbed the top of the corporate ladder, you can still better yourself. Allowing anything to stop your growth as a human being needs to be avoided. Avoided like a tree in your path as you ski down a mountain. Think about this for a moment, when someone is overly self-important do you believe they can sustain lasting relationships? I don't. They are too caught up in themselves to respect others. To show compassion. Benevolence. Or appreciation.

The first step to overcoming this malignancy is to quit taking yourself so seriously. In other words, get over yourself. When you catch yourself looking down on someone, judging someone, ridiculing someone, or dismissing someone, stop yourself. Reexamine your first inclination and make an effort to look beyond your biases. Think about how your response or preconceived notion might make the other person feel. Sometimes people get into the mindset that they can live and act however they like. But they fail to realize how impactful their words or actions can be to others. Some studies expound on the adverse effects of bullying and ridicule. These studies suggest that a majority of the victims end up carrying that abuse and ridicule self-consciously through the rest of their lives. Do you want to be responsible for that type of prolonged anguish? I don't. And I don't think you do either.

There's a saying, a person can forget what you look like, what your name was, where he worked, or several other things about you, but they will never forget how you treated them. How could they?

KEY THREE:

Be Humble

Humbleness is the true key to success. You can never be too humble. Think about this for a minute, are you more apt to help and go to bat for an arrogant "I'm smarter and better than you" type of person, or a modest "I'm not perfect so I'd be extremely grateful for your help" type of personality. There's no question, right? Humbleness wins your support hands down. It's not hard to see why either. If anyone chooses to help someone, they want to know that their efforts will be appreciated, at least on some level. Not everyone helps people to be appreciated, but they do want to feel good about helping that person.

That's a universal truth. For how important humility is, it receives very little attention. That is wrong it should be proclaimed fervently. The thing about humility is that it goes against cultural norms. People are told over and over to be confident, self-assured, proud, boastful, etc. but they are not shown how to keep these attributes in check. As I said before, it's all about moderation. There's absolutely nothing wrong with being confident, self-assured, proud, and even a little boastful (but I'm a fan of allowing others to boast for you if you deserve it). But there is something wrong if you allow these attributes to become excessive.

There is a story that encapsulates how excessive pride and self-importance hinders growth and development. A molecular biologist at the University of Pittsburgh by the name of Archer Grouse spent his life manipulating physical and chemical living matter. In the 1940s he specialized in the molecular basis of inheritance and protein synthesis. As Archer grew up he had a noble and ambitious goal of developing a vaccine for some of the world's ailments. There was one particular disease that called him more than any other polio, otherwise known as poliomyelitis. Polio was an acute viral disease that inflamed the gray matter of the spinal cord and usually caused paralysis. It was an extremely debilitating disease. Since Archer was born in 1922, he witnessed firsthand the adverse effects of polio through the Franklin Roosevelt presidency from 1933-1945. King watched as President Roosevelt's struggled to stand and function. He watched as the disease caused the mighty American politician to deteriorate and become confined to a wheelchair. Occasionally Pres. Roosevelt would grit and bear the pain and totter on metal crutches and it broke Archer's heart. He wanted to do something. Anything. To help people with this ravaging illness. So, he diligently pursued advanced education. As his knowledge and proficiency grew, his pride and self-importance bloated alongside it. He rarely talked or converse with people below his educational level. They were insignificant in his eyes. People were to be dismissed and discounted. They could not help him in his pursuit of the vaccine for polio. Nor could they carry a conversation with him that would be interesting, he believed. Even family and friends felt snubbed by his arrogance. Colleagues intentionally avoided him. Archer found himself striving arduously for data that could easily be obtained from others. But his personality kept them from sharing freely with him. Archer's goal came from a good place, to help others, but in the process of reaching it, he lost his humility. In his arrogance, he could not stand people. Particularly uneducated people. And that hindered him immensely. Humility allows you to believe you don't always have the right answer. That you aren't a perfect person. That there's always room for growth and understanding. And that every person, no matter who they are or how educated, can teach you something. Archer failed to conceptualize this fact. And because of that, he missed the chance to connect with Henry Smith, a janitor at the University of Pittsburgh. Henry had no formal education beyond the sixth grade. He grew up dirt poor and was forced to quit school early due to the depression in the need to support his family. Henry cleaned the laboratory wing where Archer was trying to find the vaccine for polio. He also cleans many other laboratories within the University. During his cleaning duties, he would constantly try to engage the scientists in the various labs to share their studies with him. Henry had an inquisitive mind. He loved to learn from studious scholars. But there was one scholar that refused to give him even a bare-boned explanation of his work: Archer Grouse. There were over 100 scientists and only Archer could not see past Henry's education level and job. He viewed Henry as a peasant. A loser. Not someone worth the time to share his work with. It was a fateful mistake. Archer's arrogance prevented the development of a polio vaccine for many years. See, Archer was approaching polio by developing gamma globulin, which was blood plasma containing antibodies, taken from polio survivors. The problem with this method was they could not be adequately replicated because of the limited availability of plasma. To overcome this problem Archer was busy trying to find a solution that did not include plasma. He tried to figure out a way to feasibly grow antibodies. But he was completely stumped. He didn't know how to do it. The tragedy of the situation, though, is his haughtiness prevented him from reaching out to others. In his mind, he rationalized that if he couldn't figure it out no one could. It was pure unadulterated arrogance. And it prolonged the pain and suffering of polio victims for two more years. Due to complete aggravation and frustration, Archer gave up in 1950. He believed growing a vaccine would be impossible. And due to the repulsion people felt about him no one dissuaded him from quitting. The unfortunate thing is, he was close. So very close, in fact, that when a new scientist by the name of Jonas Salk came along it didn't take very long at all to solve the puzzle. And he solved it with the help of an unlikely source Henry Smith, the uneducated janitor. Henry had been exposed to years of novel and unique experiments through his inquisitive nature. Most scientists were eager to exhibit their experimental prowess to a layperson like Henry. One particular experiment from a long-retired scientist came to mind when Jonas Salk discussed his dilemma with Henry late one night. Through Jonas's humility to disclose the problem, Henry suggested the unique process of growing the antibodies in monkey kidney tissue culture (otherwise known as Vero cell line). The suggestion was monumental! Within two years Jonas Salk developed the "Salk Vaccine"! The vaccine would go on to provide the antibodies to combat polio in 90% of all participants after two doses and against all three types of polio. It was a huge breakthrough 99% of all participants became immune after three doses. How crazy is that! Along with the future vaccine called the "Sabin Vaccine" polio has been eradicated by 99% worldwide. See how far a little humility would have gone! This parable, even if it could be untrue, shines a bright light on the power of humility. Being able to recognize your weaknesses and reaching out to others is an asset to be valued not ridiculed. Nurture humility. Foster it and all you do, others will recognize it, and naturally gravitate toward you.

I am a picture-perfect example of this truism. See, there is nothing more intimidating than trying to do something you have no clue how to do. Facing a feat such as that takes a lot of humility. And that's exactly what I had when writing my books. I had no idea how to write. How to articulate anything. Create anything. Or do any other technical writing. Yet, I sucked my pride up and reached out. Presenting my weakness to others. Sharing my deficiency endeared me to them. They in turn wanted to help. They wanted to fill my weaknesses with their expertise.

It did not always go the way I projected it either. I got a lot of doors slammed in my face before I found the team to develop my books. My first attempt was a failure. I paid a media company to help my book with marketing. It was agreed that I pay $10,000 for this service. Keep in mind I didn't have a dime. I agreed despite my lack of funds. I worked hard to come up with the money-selling pre-order books I toiled arduously for it. Forgoing all non-necessary expenses paid by the media company. Looking back now, I realize how naïve I was. Putting all my faith, money, and hope in a company that sole purpose was to profit was a huge mistake. But not only that, it gave me a false sense of confidence. I found myself believing the books were going to be marketed relatively easily. What a fool I was. I didn't know how much time, effort, and expertise went into an endeavor like the one I was pursuing. The media company did, but they had a financial interest in keeping me ignorant of the true costs. Their goal was to string me along until they had milked me for as much money as possible. Their media company did not have the expertise or capabilities to market my books. From the beginning, they were scamming me. I did not have adequate knowledge of what it took to advertise and market books I was taking advantage of. I did not come to the realization immediately that this was happening, but it slowly dawned on me. But by that time, I was out $5000. It was a tragic event, but it taught me a valuable lesson. It taught me to be more vigilant. To avoid proudly assuming others had my interests at heart. I should have conducted more of the investigation before blindly trusting. No matter what though, I learned lessons, and that is what life is about. I am disappointed I lost that money. But I know everything happened for a reason. The most important thing, however, is that I remained humble. I took this fraud in stride. Sure, I consulted an attorney regarding my legal options but it was not done in anger but in redress.

THE ART OF LIVING

DANIEL SIMMS

KEY FOUR:

Banish Vanity and Materialism

DANIEL SIMMS

People are so focused on appearances that they lose sight of what others are attracted to. I always find it amazing when I see someone caught up excessively in vanity. Others may initially be interested in someone due to their appearance. But that does not last long. What does last is depth, sincerity, and genuineness. Your personality is what is important. Your appearance should not be center stage. The thing with excessive vanity is it clouds your perception of the world around you. You cannot adequately address others if you are completely focused on yourself. People can sense immediately if you are that way, so it clouds their perception of you too. So not only are you self-sabotaging yourself, you are creating a barrier between you and others.

That is terrible. Let us avoid this trap. There are many forms of vanity that we need to watch for. I say "we" because I am just as prone to vanity as the next person. This is a human condition, not a unique attribute isolated to certain individuals.

Many people believe vanity only extends to exterior appearances. This is very untrue. The fact is vanity can also be a mentality. Sure, exterior appearances get most of the credit when it comes to describing vanity. But it should not be that way.

Let me give you an example. I had a friend, let's call him John, he was one of the cool guys. He was incarcerated for dealing drugs. But of course, he got locked up when he built an extremely profitable drug business. He had unlimited finances to spoil himself. And he did. Excessively. He would pay hundreds for fancy haircuts that were in style. Thousands for every expensive pair of shoes he could get his hands on. His closet was filled with name-brand clothes. His neck and fingers were adorned with gold. He had many cars and each one had a booming sound system. Needless to say, he was living it up. He attended all the local events. Went to all the popular clubs, bars, and meeting places. He was invited to all the house parties. People hung around him tirelessly due to his extravagant lifestyle. They enjoy the benefits of him throwing his wealth around town. They did not like John for who he was, they liked him for what he could do for them. They were superficial friends. And John was a superficial person so he could not look through their false façade.

Ultimately, the party had to come to an end for John. A confidential informant infiltrated this organization and took him down. He was charged, taken to trial, and sentenced within months of his arrest. All his material wealth was seized. He was left with nothing but his personality. And that was a shallow puddle at the beginning of summer. His fair-weather friends shook him like a leaf. He was quickly forgotten by everyone. His eight-year sentence should have been called a life sentence by the way his acquaintances abandoned him. Throughout his incarceration, he dwelt on dreams of grandeur. Occasionally he would have a moment of clarity and resolve to start a new legitimate life upon release. But very little time and energy was spent on solidifying this goal. Instead, most of his time and energy was spent working out, socializing, and playing cards. He maintained his materialistic and vain personality throughout. Needless to say, his sentence flew by. He had no plan for his reintegration. We had a conversation before he released about his future. I wanted to impart my wisdom. So, I did. I explained that inmates return to prison within three years. The most effective way to circumvent that destiny is to focus on finding a job. No matter where it's at, as a matter of fact, I recommend applying to McDonald's, Burger King, or some other fast-food joint. Unsurprisingly, he took my advice indignantly. He was too good to work the low-brow occupation of fast food. So, I asked what he was qualified to do then. He had no answer because he had no qualifications. All he knew was he was better than a fast job. He was stuck in his superficiality. He could not bring himself to look past it. Eventually, he got out with this mentality. He refused to work in fast food yet that was the only occupation he was qualified for. He could have easily started at fast food, received training or education, or another occupation. But he didn't. He turned that down. He spent very little time looking for a job he spent more time focusing on his appearance and talking to women. His vanity pursuits led him to need money immediately. So, he went back to the only thing he knew. Drug dealing. Within months he was back in prison with a 15-year sentence. When I saw him again his personality was finally changing, and he recognized his errors.

But it was too late. That is the moral of this story. Do not be so stuck on yourself, on your appearance, or your material wealth. Those things are superficial. Hollow. And meaningless. What is important is you. Your future. Your personality. Those things will remain with you forever. So let us pledge to banish our vain and materialistic attributes. That way we can focus on ourselves.

KEY FIVE:

Quit Taking Yourself So Serious, Have Fun, Get Excited, And Think of Others

DANIEL SIMMS

THE ART OF LIVING

Do you wake up each morning in anticipation or trepidation? That answer reflects your mindset. If your thoughts are stuck in the past or in some possible future hardship, you're going to lose the greatest blessing of all and that is the present moment!

Lower your defenses do not put so much pressure on yourself. You need to get out of the mistaken belief that you have to constantly be so serious. That life is not going to forgive you if you make a mistake. The thing is life goes on whether you are humorless and somber or fun-loving and free. Life is crazy like that. It is going to unfold how it is supposed to. No matter how much you stress and agonize over something.

So my advice is to quit taking yourself so seriously. You are not the arbiter of fate. No one is. Make no mistake I do not espouse neglect. But I do propose allowing yourself to enjoy life. If you don't take the initiative and truly get over the falsehood that life is difficult then you will exist in perpetual difficulty.

It's that you are only in control of yourself. Therefore, you cannot dictate how people will react or how events will unfold.

That is not your domain. Since this is a fact, you have a decision to make, are you going to continue a flawed perspective or embark on a new point of view? I hope you elect the new viewpoint because once you do life will open up with possibilities. So instead of missing your kid's softball game to finish a report on corporate earnings put the report on hold and enjoy your child. Take a day off in the winter to go sledding. Or go have a snowball fight.

I give you the license have fun! Now go! Remember when the world had so much promise and luster that you were excited about facing it? That outlook is still inside you. Even if it has slowly faded it is there. Trust me on that. All you have to do is find it. So, find it. Once you have found yourself start sharing yourself with others. You are not an island. You can make a difference if you truly want to. So do it. Others need you to show them the peace you have found. Do not hold it inside because if you do it will eat you up inside. Knowing how pointless it was to exist in empty pursuits and faulty thought processes should propel you to help others recognize it too.

There was a study recently by a university that confirmed something I have known for a long time. That it is better to give than to receive. Measuring the synapses in the brain they were able to determine with absolute certainty that the reward center was triggered more completely upon giving than receiving.

How remarkable is that! Conventional wisdom would have us believe we would respond more favorably to receiving than giving but that plainly is not true. Our psychological response does not lie. So, the next time you can be charitable, take it! Even if it is from a purely selfish standpoint. You will benefit from it. Trust me on that. Do not hesitate, put these suggestions to practice today!

THE ART OF LIVING

KEY SIX:

Quit Making Excuses

DANIEL SIMMS

On so many levels I identify with this. I had to add "quit making excuses" because I find myself falling victim to it all the time. I see others doing it too. So I had to add a chapter that specifically addressed it. I believe each one of us has the inclination to make excuses and that just means it's a human problem. But all problems are meant to be solved. So let us solve it.

The best way to overcome anything is by recognizing you have an issue first. Once that is done the actual work can begin. When I first addressed it myself, I tried an experiment. I decided to follow through with whatever I needed to do without hesitation. That means if something needed to be done it was done. Period. My previous mentality would always leave room to slack. "Oh, I'll do it later". "I've got a day off in a few days, I'll do it then". The excuses were endless. And they could go on indefinitely sometimes. Things might never get done if I continued to foster that attitude. But luckily, I recognized it and experimented on how to overcome it. At first, it was frustrating to follow through with everything so quickly. I could be laying there in bed reflecting on the day, before going to sleep, and a thought will pop into my mind. A letter I was supposed to send or an email I was supposed to compose; thereby, causing me to get up immediately and do it. It was frustrating. But eventually, it was exhilarating.

It opened up my future considerably. And it made me exceedingly productive and that made me extremely happy.

How happy would you be to know everything you need to do is done? That way whatever comes your way in the future can be addressed immediately. Without vying for your attention along with other projects. How awesome is that?

There is a well-known way to establish any new habit like the one I am proposing. And that is to do it for seven days straight. After seven days it has been proven a new habit can form. So consciously decide to accomplish anything and everything that you take on. This process also seems to put things under a microscope too. You'll no longer blindly agree to take on everything that comes your way. You will know if you can do it or not due to what you have going on. I like that fact because it gives the world clarity that might never have been there. Before I set about doing this experiment my world was chaotic. I never knew if something was being neglected or not because everything was put off until the last moment.

I hated that feeling of anxiety. Don't you? Is it not time to address it by mentally determining that nothing will be neglected anymore? It's a liberating experience and I hope you get to experience it.

THE ART OF LIVING

KEY SEVEN:

Solidify Your Dream into a Clearly Defined Goal

THE ART OF LIVING

I don't know how many times someone has come up and talked to me about their ideas and dreams. I welcome it. I love stoking the flames of creativity. I believe everyone has the potential to achieve great things. And if I can help them in any way, I want to. Most of the time people just want validation or confirmation. If I can give that to them I will.

The problem arises, however, when it comes to execution. People can come up with ideas and dreams, but very rarely can they follow through with them. That is where this chapter comes in. The best way to make anything come to fruition is by clearly defining it. What is it you want to achieve? What is the most outlandish idea or dream you have? Is it feasible? Most of us cannot start a space company so that is not feasible. But most of us can start a business. Write a book. Or climb a mountain. It's all about dedication and resolve. But before you can even have that you have settled on what your goal is.

So what is your goal? I'm not referring to a simple task. I'm talking about what you would be proud of accomplishing

20 years from now. A long-term dream of yours. What is it? Clearly articulate it. Write it down right now. Take a minute to do it. Then get it printed in fancy script on elaborate card stock paper; lastly, have it framed. Put it somewhere you can see it every day. If you are forced to see it every day you will consciously make more effort to achieve it. To achieve it you have to take many steps but the first step is identifying the goal. And once that is done the rest of the way to achieving it should be transparent. You should know what will be needed to at least start heading in the goal's direction.

Like Albert Einstein said: "If A equals success, then the formula is A equals X plus Y plus Z. X is work. Y is play. Z is keep your mouth shut."

Or Dwight D. Eisenhower said: "We succeed only as we identify in life, or in war, or in anything else, a single overriding objective, and make all other considerations bend to that one objective."

See the most important thing to do is identify the goal. The objective. And the next thing to do is determine the formula or steps to get there. I had to do it in my life. I had many dreams, but they were only dreams. Most of them came to nothing. They were pipedreams. Unless I sat down and clearly defined, they would evaporate like the dew by mid-morning. It was sad. Looking back now I realized the error of my ways. But luckily, I finally decided upon one goal and that was to write "Hopeless in Seattle, A Foster Kid's Manifesto." And I accomplished it. Then I was onto the next goal. Which was this book. The beauty of setting goals is it solidifies the idea. I love that because it almost makes it tangible. Realistic. And reachable. Which it is. Anything you set your mind to you can achieve. I have faith in you. All there is to it is to do it. That's it.

In my case, once I gathered the confidence to start pursuing my goal of being an author, I found it relatively straightforward. It seems the first step of setting the goal was where I met the most mental resistance. I believe the doubts and insecurities about facing such a feat were my worst enemy. But once I faced them it was downhill. Smooth sailing. And I'm positive it will be the same for you. Trust me on that.

Another fascinating thing I came to realize when I accomplished my first book was the sheer confidence it instilled. Once the book was done, I knew that my dreams were possible; therefore, it propelled me to make new goals. And with the newly instilled confidence, I pursued them with vigor.

That can be you. That is you! All you have to do is set the path. The goal. And the direction and it will all come together if you pursue it. This I promise you.

I invite you to share your goal with our website. On our social media pages. On your social media pages. The best thing you can do is broadcast your defined goal. That way others can hold you accountable for it. They can support your efforts with positive reinforcement. Whatever you need to accomplish your dreams is available to you, all you need to do is go after it.

DANIEL SIMMS

KEY EIGHT:

Leap Into Action

Why wait? That is my question to you. Is there any valid excuse to do so? If your goal is defined you have a direction. So quit procrastinating and go after it. I don't mean to be abrupt and matter of fact but it's just the way it is. You have to leap into action to get things done. There is no room for waiting. You can always do something to get closer to your goals. Sure, there may be legitimate things that hinder our pursuits but they should not stop it. Ever. There is a book you can read. A webinar to watch. Or a mentor to confer with. There is always some type of activity you could be doing to get closer to accomplishing more dreams. Never accept inaction because that breeds stagnation. Standing still is not an option. Only moving forward should be considered. Period. Anything else is counterproductive. Think about this, when you start a chess game do you make a couple of moves and stop for a while? No, of course not, that would only cause you to forget your methodology for your previous moves. The same goes for reaching your goals. The moment you start slacking and putting it off you will be putting yourself at a disadvantage. Who wants that? Not me. And hopefully not you either. So let us resolve to not do that. We need to adopt the mind frame that every day is an opportunity. It is either a step closer to your dreams or a step backward. The option is ours. No one will reach your dream for you. That much is a reality. But what else is a reality is that someone might achieve their dreams, which may so happen to be the same dreams as yours. Dreams and even goals do not have copyright protections. Anyone can pursue them. Your destiny is not assured unless you take action to bring it to fruition. You can be positive about that. And you can also be positive that someone somewhere might reach that destiny before you. If that happens, how saddened would you be? Take that conception of sadness and use it to impel you towards taking action.

Leonardo da Vinci was quoted as saying: "O' Lord, Thou givest us everything, at a price of effort." Another quote I like is by Richard Cabot: "Work is doing what you now enjoy for the sake of a future which you clearly see and desire. Drudgery is doing under strain what you don't now enjoy and for no end that you can now appreciate."

My favorite, however, is by Jack Valenti: "A widely prevalent notion today seems to demand instant achievement of goals, without any of the wearying, frustrating preparation that is indispensable to any task. As the exemplar of a way of life, the professional man or woman who injects every new task for duty, no matter how small, with the discipline of mind and spirit is a vanishing America, particularly among those who too often believe that dreams come true because they ought to and not because they are caused to materialize."

You have to take the hard arduous steps required to meet any goal no matter how small. We are designed to have dreams and aspirations but reaching them is not always easy. It does take hard work sometimes. Don't let that deter you. Hard work will only make you appreciate achievement more.

We are all given the blessing of unique thought. Most of us also can reach whatever we put our minds to. Most times the distractions of life bog us down so we lose sight of our dreams. We can't let that happen. Your goal is worth reaching. Your efforts are worth expending. You have something to contribute to the world and I implore you to take it. Sure, it might be hard to reach it, and you might get fatigued on the way, but in the end, you will be so happy you did it. You will not regret your efforts. But you will regret it if you don't. It might not hit you today, tomorrow, or next week, but someday you will look back with pain and regret for not pursuing your dreams.

Nothing is worth abandoning your dreams. Not your job. Not more relationships. Not anything. You can find ways to fit your pursuit into your life. No matter what. If you are of the mind that you can't then you need to revert to chapter 6, quit making excuses!

If I can overcome the handicaps of incarceration, lack of education, and lack of support then you can overcome anything too. I believe the most important thing we have is tenacity. Each of us is endowed with this beautiful trait and it can propel us into some incredible places. All you need to do is harness it. Think about all those people that would have failed had they not harnessed tenacity. Steve Jobs. Bill Gates. Thomas Edison. The list could go on and on. They had dreams that turned into goals that turned into actions that eventually turned into something big. We all have that potential. Every single one of us. It is our job to merely seize it!

So, get to seizing it!

What are you waiting for?

Leap into action.

THE ART OF LIVING

KEY NINE:

Ignorance is not bliss, Education is!

DANIEL SIMMS

THE ART OF LIVING

I have done so much thought on the maxim "Ignorance is bliss" and I've determined it is untrue. It is not bliss. It's nothing close to that. At most, it is an illusion of bliss. Being unable to address the complex world around you is not a good thing at all. It is a hardship. Pitted with many disadvantages. The sooner you realize this the better.

    I remember one time when I interacted with a judge and how inadequate I felt after the exchange. I was arguing my position about sovereignty and my absolute rights as a human being. The judge was able to easily bat down my uneducated arguments. No matter how I articulated my words it seemed she had a counter for them. It was frustrating. But at the same time, it was enlightening. It proved to be a pivotal moment for me in my journey. I thought I was so smart. I had adopted a sophisticated philosophy that I believe explains how the US government incarcerated so many of its citizens. I was sold on it. But I failed to adequately investigate the claims the proponents of the sovereignty movement espoused. Therefore, I was at an extreme disadvantage versus a skilled jurist that studied law.

I could have taken the exchange lightly and forgotten it but that is not in my DNA. It propelled me to seek a deeper understanding of the law and myself. So, I proceeded to educate myself on both. I spent hours reading case law. Taking paralegal courses. And writing essays on my positions. I remember spending a month writing a brief arguing my interpretation of the law. It was arduous work. In the end, however, I was a bona fide paralegal. I graduated from an educational institution, but the real learning came from my hours of self-propelled investigations. I would not trade those hours of self-development for anything. They were invaluable. The same will go for you. I have never regretted reading a book. But I have regretted not doing so.

Ultimately, you want to step into every situation with the knowledge to effectively handle it. When you are starting a new business read everything you can about that industry. Educate yourself on the competitors. Learn about ways to convincingly convey your company's message through marketing and advertising. And if you're serious about your entrepreneurship maybe you should pursue a conventional degree in business. That way as your learning the subject matter you can apply it to your business.

How awesome is that? And the idea that you can only pursue education when it pertains to your business, job, career, or industry is just plain wrong. The fact is whatever you have an inkling of interest in learning you should pursue it. Period. Colleges do not teach a wide diverse curriculum for anything. There is a methodology behind it. Knowing disparate topics enables you to converse and articulate messages more effectively. It also lends you the authority to do so. You never know when the knowledge will come in handy. But I'm sure it will someday. There is a time and place for everything.

Wisdom is gathered over years and years of seeking. You cannot wake up every day with the specialized knowledge to code a social media website. You have to study computer programming before that is possible. Specialized knowledge is extremely valuable. It cannot be adequately measured or quantified. To specialize in anything demands respect. And do not be confused, I am not specifically referring to conventional industries or sectors either. If you have spent years amassing friends on Facebook, followers on Twitter, and subscribers on YouTube then you are an expert on social media.

Some companies would spend thousands to replicate that for their business. Or if you have a passion for football and creating fantasy football teams then that should be considered specialization. You could easily parlay that knowledge to advise others on how to play fantasy football. The fantasy football niche is booming. What I'm saying is never stop learning. Pursue every educational opportunity possible. Time is a gift, use it to expand your mind; instead of squandering it in front of a screen.

Take me for example, I am surrounded by individuals that are intentionally trying to waste their time, their sole focus is getting through their prison sentence. On the other hand, my sole focus is on learning everything I can. I could easily get lost in television, gambling, and exercising like others, but I made a conscious decision not to. And that decision set the tone for my whole life. No matter if I spend the next couple of decades incarcerated or I get out this year I will continue striving for enlightenment. I have already learned enough specialized skills to make a fortune in the real world.

I am proficient in writing, business, law, stock market trading, computer programming, video game design, accounting, and even cooking. Some of these I took complete courses on and some I learned through diligent study. Honestly, I'm convinced it doesn't make a difference how you arrive at your specialization. As long as you get there. I believe the key, however, is having the drive and passion to put in the time and energy to get there. So many people think there is an easy road, but the fact is nothing is worth fighting for more than wisdom. When I first learned computer programming I did it because it intrigued me. The prison I was at offered a unique course on programming in videogame design that appealed to me. Most people in my situation would refuse to learn an occupation that might never be utilized due to a long prison sentence. My sentence, as it sits right now, it's not even half done and I'm over 10 years into it. On paper, I got 24 years left. It's quite possible computer programming in videogame design will evolve considerably in those years making my skills obsolete. But I don't care. I still wanted the knowledge. The same goes for the bookkeeping/accounting degree. Who is going to hire a repeat criminal like me to balance their company's books? No one. So that accounting knowledge and nine months of diligence classwork are essentially useless to me. But I could care less. Sure, some may argue that since I am incarcerated all I have is time to spend, and in the free world, time is more valuable. I believe that is a cop-out. Prison is a microcosm of the outside world. It encompasses all levels of distraction and responsibilities as the outside world. It is easy to squander time outside as it is inside. It all boils down to perspective and outlook. If you are a student of life, you'll be one whether you're incarcerated or in the White House. It makes no difference; you can always make time for educational pursuits that much I am positive about.

As Plato said, "...Knowledge is food for the soul..."

There is a Chinese proverb that says, "Learning is a treasure that will follow its owner everywhere". In other words, no one can ever take it away from you. It's yours forever. For someone like me accustomed to not having much that means a lot. I love that I can be stripped bare, which I have on multiple occasions, and still harbor the knowledge I worked hard for.

One thing I have found out over the years is that it's important to recognize when you don't know something. And when you recognize that, to have the initiative to learn it. Whatever it is. For instance, I don't know how many times I have read a book and an unknown word popped up. The first thing I do when I see it is open a dictionary. I have multiple dictionaries. One for each area of study. Law. Computer programming. Financial and investment. Banking. I've got dictionaries for each. I know and understand I cannot learn any topic effectively unless I dig deep and understand what words mean. This practice applies to everything. If you need or want to learn something don't procrastinate just do it. Take the initiative. Like George Simmel said, "He is educated who knows how to find out what he doesn't know."

THE ART OF LIVING

KEY TEN:

Diligence and Hard Labor Leads to Happiness

The beauty of diligent labor is that it produces. What it produces is truly endless. The sky is not the limit. Think about all the wonderful things that have been created through it. You can have a million inventive ideas that could change the world dramatically, but if you don't have the diligence to make them come to fruition then they are useless. Empty dreams are not worth the air they play across. Dreams are beautiful, they can inspire creative things, but dreams are also mirages that can delude one into a false state of contentment. If all you have is your dreams, then you have nothing. 100% of nothing is still nothing.

It is the action, the diligent hard labor that produces the wonders of the world. Not the dreams. Dreams are a critical part of the equation, but the work is what brings dreams to life. Dreams are lifeless, devoid of the capability to come alive. Without you, they are doomed.

So, if you have dreams that you turned into a clearly defined goal and took action at making it happen through educating yourself or various other methods, then it's time to put in the hard work!

Hard diligent labor is what makes dreams come true. Nothing else. Don't bank on charity or gifts. Bank only on yourself. Because you can do whatever you put your mind to. And I sincerely mean that. I have a foster father that has been incredibly impactful in my life. He owns Seattle tree service and one piece of advice he gave me hit home for me. He told me no matter what I'm doing, whom I'm doing it for, or what I'm being paid, to always work hard at it. Even if I'm scrubbing scum off a garbage can with no one looking I need to put my all into it. When I first received this critical wisdom, I did not necessarily gather the deep significance of it. Over time I came to discover how important it is.

I believe you will recognize throughout your life that if you apply yourself good things will happen. Ultimately, this book is about finding freedom and success. And to find them you need to put sweat equity into it.

Freedom and success are abstractions but trust me they become tangible. There is value in putting forth the effort to reach the goals you seek. Even if the going gets tough continue striving towards it, and you will be surprised by what you can accomplish.

One thing I am positive about is you will never regret putting forth effort. Certain circumstances might cause you to regret why you put forth the effort. But the effort itself can never be regretted as that is where work ethics come from. Whether you like what the effort is expended for or not does not matter. All that matters is that you are establishing the practice of diligent work labor. Once this is firmly entrenched in your psyche then the world is yours for the picking. You will be ahead of the pack. No one will be able to detract from your success either because you will have earned it. I promise you will come to cherish the journey as much as the rewards. Continue onward!

THE ART OF LIVING

KEY ELEVEN:

**Discern Fact from Fiction through Data
And Learn from Mistakes**

DANIEL SIMMS

THE ART OF LIVING

How many times have you or someone you know reacted without all the facts? It happens all the time in prison. I recall one incident in particular as a prime example. In prison, most inmates are there because someone told on them. Therefore, if someone shows up with a "snitch jacket" then it goes without saying they will be targeted for violence. Or at the very least they will be ostracized. Anyway, a guy showed up on the chain bus one day and within moments of hitting the mainline, there was a vicious rumor going around. Allegedly the guy told on someone in the county jail and supposedly he was even in the newspaper doing it. Wow! Think about how explosive this revelation was! It was traveling at the speed of sound throughout the institution. Everyone knew the story before the guy had even made his bed. People were pointing him out like he had Ebola.

Imagine this guy's poor luck. He did not even know a rumor was started, let alone thriving, regarding him. He tried to introduce himself to others but they rebuffed him rudely. In the chow hall, he meekly went from table to table asking to sit down to eat and each table rebuked him. It was sad. But it was also the nature of prison. No one said it was going to be easy. After a couple of days of feeling the pressure of cold looks and sharp rejection the guy tried to reach out to others. He humbly approached a group of inmates gathered around the basketball court and asked them what the deal was. He came prepared, bringing his judgments and sentence, showing them, he was in for a "solid case". Which means not a rape or sex case. Nevertheless, the group still snubbed him by telling him they did not care what he was in for, they still did not want anything to do with him. It was useless for him to continue pleading with them, so he changed tactics and cussed them out. It was a big mistake. The guy received a group beat down. He didn't even have a chance. It was pitiful. What really made it sad, however, was that the guy was not a snitch at all. Everyone had jumped to the wrong conclusion. His name was vaguely similar to the guy in the newspaper but that's it. He was merely serving a drug sentence. There was no one told on in his case at all. If people would have given him the benefit of the doubt and allowed him to show his paperwork they may have noticed he was not even from the city the newspaper covered. It was a complete mistaken identity. In the real world, this wisdom is just as applicable. People go off reacting to things all the time without an adequate understanding of the circumstances. And it's a shame. The proper way to do it is to gather all the facts first and once all the data is in them decipher it. Take action on things only after you have determined the right course based on the data. This is applicable in business.

In social situations. In almost every facet of civilization. Learning from data sets is extremely practical and worth implementing in your life immediately. Another important thing, and this should go without saying, learn from your mistakes.

Don't be a fool and neglect life's experiential gift of mistakes. Learn from them. Write them down. Never forget. History always repeats itself, so if you have an invaluable experience that might save you or someone you know that is a gift. A blessing. So why not keep them at the forefront of your mind? You might not run into the same dilemma today, tomorrow, or next week, but someday it will come. So don't neglect mistakes, they are life's precious lessons. Take them and harbor them in your mind's eye. When I first came to prison, I was walking down a tier and as I passed a cell, I absentmindedly looked inside it. It was a cursory look that might have lasted two or three seconds. But I did this to a cell where two people were looking out onto the tier, so they caught me gazing. Keep in mind I'm young, a little past my 19th birthday. To say prison was an intimidating environment would be an understatement. My senses were on high alert. The two individuals in the cell were in their mid-30s. Both were covered with tattoos. And were extremely muscular. Imagine my apprehension when they called me over to the bars of their cell. When I got there, he looked me straight in the eyes and asked me a question.

"Did you drop something?"

I was so new to prison life that I thought he was trying to be helpful. He did not have a cold or mean look on his face, so I responded carefully and pleasantly.

"Nope, I'm just on my way to the yard."

"Oh yeah then why the hell are you looking in my cell!" he said vehemently.

He went from peaceful to antagonistic within seconds. It was quite a lesson. I learned not to look in other's cells. And this is a practical lesson I learned through experience. The fact is, in prison, you don't want to know anything that is not your business. People are getting busted constantly in prison for various things and the last thing you want to be is suspected of telling on them.

Therefore, if you understand that, you don't want to be looking into anyone's cell. They could be doing anything in there. From tattooing. Using drugs. Or fighting. Anything. So why would I not accept and cherish this tidbit of wisdom? Use it to survive the hostile prison environment. So that is exactly what I did. Needless to say, I never looked in another cell that did not belong to me again. Period. Take my advice, it was a lesson well learned.

THE ART OF LIVING

DANIEL SIMMS

THE ART OF LIVING

KEY TWELVE:

Focus all your time, energy, and resources

DANIEL SIMMS

When I am distracted or unfocused whatever I am working on always suffers. Does that happen to you? It is believed because we all have remnants of our primitive mind still encoded deep within, we are most effective when we focus on one thing at a time. Which makes sense. I am sure many people can multitask quite well but are they producing at a high level, that much is unclear. I find it best to focus my attention on one thing at a time. I can do many things throughout the day, but it takes actual concentration, time, and resources to focus solely on them. That way I am positive I am producing the best. That goes for everything in my life. When I am working out, I refuse to be distracted by socializing. And when it comes to writing I choose to block everything out and put myself in a trancelike zone. That is the only way I can focus completely, otherwise, I may find myself straying.

Whenever you take on too many projects you are diluting your work. Do you want to do that? I don't. I would rather be an effective producer than an ineffective one. That should go without saying. Right? So, the answer is to commit yourself to focus. Focusing your time. Focusing your mind. Focusing your energy. Focusing your resources.

To do this you need to prioritize. There will be some things that need to be excluded from your life. You might not be able to watch television much. Or interact on social media. Only you know what has to be cut. But I am sure something does.

There is a prison story that will bring this chapter to life. Every week a chain bus delivers inmates from all over the state. Like clockwork, they come into the prison with doe-like eyes or jaded demeanors. Most grapple with the negative atmosphere by trying to fit in. This entails constantly proving yourself essentially assimilating to prison culture. This is a common strategy. Anyway, on one particular chain, two inmates showed up. Both had nearly identical sentences: 20 years. When I talked with them, they were still relatively new. They had been there for about a week. Both seemed to have some intelligence about them. Which is not always the case in prison. But one of them named Dustin had gone to college for a year. When we got to discuss their plans while incarcerated the other guy, Jeremy, was quite adamant he was going to focus completely on his criminal appeal so he could go home early. Dustin was likewise committed to his appeal too. Over the months I saw the level of dedication between divert. Dustin became mired in the prison culture and spent less and less time in the law library. While Jeremy focused all his time, energy, and resources solely on his appeal. Jeremy had no formal education further than eighth grade. While Dustin had made it to college. I must admit I would have bet on Dustin before Jeremy regarding their dedication. But I was wrong. Despite his lack of formal education, Jeremy has something Dustin did not have, which was a focus. Jeremy filed a new petition or motion every month. He refused to be sidetracked by the prison culture. And he was rewarded for his dedication. Within two years he had won a new trial. He had achieved his goal. By focusing completely on it he succeeded! I remember standing next to Dustin while Jeremy was being loaded back on the chain bus. He was on the way back to County jail for a retrial. Dustin had this look of pure defeat. Maybe it was due to his failure or inadequacy, I don't know, but he was sad. I recall dwelling on that moment many times. There was a clear contrast between the two individuals. One was focused and driven. The other was distracted and double-minded. That contracting experience has stayed with me for obvious reasons. This, of course, is an extreme example of neglect and inattention. But it encapsulates the essence of the chapter. If you want something focus on it.

KEY THIRTEEN:

Be Original, Imaginative, and Innovative

DANIEL SIMMS

There are too many people in this world that are mediocre. Do not be one of them. Be yourself whatever that may look like. There is no right or wrong way to be. Sure, the world wants to put you in a box. It wants to easily define you and your personality. Why let it?

Make it harder for others to box you in. The thing is, it might appear hard to be original and stand out, but over time people will respect you and come to envy your pioneering spirit. There are countless stories of unique people achieving great heights due to their imaginative personalities. The world may want to put you in a box but the moment you step out of it and shatter their preconceived notion of who you are, you become an enigma.

In prison stereotyping is rampant. Authorities constantly want to put inmates in a box. It's like they need inmates to act according to their preconceived conceptions. That way they can excuse their culpability in perpetuating a failed system of mass incarceration. When inmates exhibit acts of genuine compassion, empathy, and kindness, authorities are quick to charge the intimate with manipulation or some other ulterior motive. As if this inmate is not a human. It is sad. This type of behavior only disincentives inmates from being kind. You exhibit genuine kindness and receive skepticism and unbelief it is extremely disheartening. Prison authorities are in a position of power that can be used constructively or destructively. And currently, the prevailing mentality is destructive. Which is terrible. Not all inmates are incorrigible. Most inmates have more depth to them than just antisocial behavior. All they need is encouragement and help. That's it. There are ways to foster and facilitate inmates' unique personalities without stifling their rehabilitation.

So, on a macro level, there needs to be a mentality shift by prison authorities. Currently, they put inmates in a box and color them with a wide brush of pessimism and doubt. That is the worst thing to do. Expectations have an uncanny way of self-fulfilling themselves. If you expect someone to act and behave a certain way, you can usually find something to match your expectations. On a micro level, I have experienced the hardship of being targeted for my uniqueness. Constantly looking for positive ways to destroy stereotypes is not a value attribute in prison. Not by authorities or inmates. It is a chronic epidemic to disparage positive developments. I guess this is because of the prison environment's status quo. People want to be validated in their assumption and the assumption is that inmates are incorrigible. Destroying that image of inmates is hard. Yet I still pursue it. I work on myself, and I encourage those around me that are interested in self-development too. That way I can affect the change without relying on others. I enjoy being a positive influence in a negative environment.

On an intellectual level being able to think outside the box and be creative is incredibly valuable. Both in life generally, and business in particular. I have been able to think abstractly about many novel inventions. Not a day goes by when I am not innovating. I have even secured a patent since being incarcerated. Not to mention all the writings I have done. My mind is constantly moving. Anyone can foster creativity in themselves. There is no limit to where your imagination can take you if you only push yourself. Do not allow your current circumstances to define you. If I let that happen, I would be the quintessential inmate. But I refuse to do that. Instead, I strive to be different. To push myself to greater heights. I have the drive to be innovative and so should you. Repel stereotyping and embrace originality.

I believe the best you are is yet to come. Imagine what you could achieve if you fostered and embraced creativity. There are no words to describe your potential. Despite past hardships, current circumstances, and future outlook, you can be someone special. Strive to be unique. Shatter others' preconceived opinions of you! Don't let them put you in a box. You cannot be defined by your circumstances. Trust yourself enough to innovate. Who cares what others might think of you?

ENCAPSULATION

There are many that would disparage you in your process of self-development. It seems to be the trend nowadays. The good thing is you are aware of this tendency of others. That way when you experience it you will not be discouraged. It is not uncommon or unique for others to treat you this way. I cannot count how many people tried to disparage me in my various pursuits. At first, I took their criticisms to heart, but over time I came to realize their behavior was predictable. Others do not like to see you reach your dreams because it will remind them of their failures. They might not say it outright but subconsciously this is the truth. Over time it seems the world and life dish out a steady flow of disappointing realities. Instead of pulling themselves up by their bootstraps, they allow their past failures to prevent future progress. As this failure is the brake pedal to reaching dreams. Just because someone failed at one business, or lost one dream, that is not a blanket declaration against pursuing all the dreams in the future. Sometimes you have to fail a few times before you finally stumbled on your sweet spot. So, the next time someone disparages you and tries to discourage you, remember they are merely projecting their fears upon you.

There is no need to feed into this because it is not based on reality. Their fears are based on their failed experiences. And past failure is not a valid excuse to neglect future progress. Remember that. Internalized it. All the wisdom in the world does you no good if you do not internalize it and make it a part of who you are. You need to make the keys part of your personality. An indispensable part. So how do you do that, well you have to work on it. Make an effort at instilling them through conscious effort.

The first thing you need to realize is that it only takes seven days of repeated behavior to create a new habit. That means you only need to consciously expend seven days of effort and you will be on the road to success. There is no reason you should not begin this process immediately. You can do this by posting the 13 keys to success, quick tips reference guide on your refrigerator. Or some other easily noticed place such as your front door.

Remember to achieve the success you need to implement the keys religiously. They need to be a part of who you are. Do this by disciplining yourself to practice them daily. Once they are ingrained in your psyche, they will be a part of you then success and true freedom are yours for the taking.

Another important thing to remember is that failure is not achieved by a stroke of bad luck or one tragic event. The truth is, failure is due to several mistakes done over and over every day. Therefore, it is your job to isolate and identify those daily mistakes to reverse them. They could be mistakes in accounting, marketing, or in your thinking. Whatever they are identify them so you can overcome them.

I found over the years that the so-called educated of society are the most confused when it comes to building wealth. They think because they have a degree in engineering a fortune should fall into their lap. That could not be further from the truth. The world does not owe you riches. You have to toil and strive for that, whether your college educated or self-taught. That is a fact. You will build your wealth not from a degree, but through diligently studying your niche, and applying that knowledge to please your customers. That's it.

Before you can realize any of your dreams you need to own the present. You do this by setting aside time daily to further the dream. It needs to be a daily practice. You own the present by being productive. If you accomplish something that brings you a little closer to your dream you have owned the day. If you do not take this seriously, you'll find days slipping by with no progress. That is stagnation and it needs to be avoided at all costs. Even if you're motivated that is only enough to get your dream started. It takes discipline and habit to bring the dream to life don't forget that.

The thing is, you will never achieve any worthwhile dream or goal overnight. All you can do is work in its direction. Through persistence and tenacity, you will eventually get there. But you have to want it. You have to put in the time, energy and effort; otherwise, it is only a pipe dream that will be lost over time.

There are two realities that you will face in life. The pain of self-development and discipline. Or the pain of regretfulness. You get to choose which. But trust me on this, you will be extremely grateful later for any present effort.

Another realization I want to share with you is the power of association. There are not many profound realizations that are more important in prison. The people you surround yourself with have great influence. You might not even know this. Subconsciously people surround themselves with those they are most comfortable with. But this is not always necessarily a good thing. If all your friends are content with their station in life and have no aspirations, their spirit will rub off on you. Maybe not very much, but at least a little. You are the sum of the people you surround yourself with. If you want to reach high heights, you need to get on the shoulders of others that are higher than you. I'm not saying to ditch old friends, what I'm saying is to spend more time with those that are on the same page in life as you are. If you don't, you'll find yourself bouncing ideas, dreams, and goals off people that do not value them.

What never fails to amaze me is the millions of people that get so lost in their jobs that they lose sight of themselves. Don't do that. A job should only be a means to achieve a dream or goal, not a means to an end. Use everything, and that includes your job, to bring your goal into reality. I urge you to expend just as much effort on developing yourself as you work for others at your job. Ultimately, what it boils down to is at your job you are merely building value for others. While at the same time neglecting yourself. That is not right. You should be expending more on developing yourself than you are on developing someone else's business. Keep that in mind the next time a business matter potentially interferes with your personal endeavors.

In conclusion, I hope that I have brought you some measure of value. My goal was to part the wisdom I gather from years of incarceration. Currently, I'm in my eighteenth year of imprisonment so it should not be hard to conceptualize the incalculable amount of knowledge gathered. It is my honor and pleasure to share it with you. I know that many people would like to believe prisoners have nothing left to offer society. I believe that is a tragedy. There is immeasurable potential inside the walls of prison and hopefully, someday society recognize that.

Thirteen Keys of Success Quick Reference Guide:

1. You can be your own worst enemy, or your own best champion. But you can't be both!
2. Get over yourself! To truly love and enjoy life you need to conquer self-importance
3. Be Humble
4. Banish Vanity and Materialism
5. Quit taking yourself so seriously, have fun, get excited, and think of others
6. Quit making excuses
7. Solidify your dream into a clearly defined goal
8. Leap into action
9. Ignorance is not bliss, education is!
10. Diligence and hard labor leads to happiness
11. Discern fact from fiction through data and learn from mistakes
12. Focus all your time, energy, and resources
13. Be original, imaginative, and innovative

The "I Learned in Prison Movement"

People are so quick to disregard and discredit inmates and ex-felons as if they have nothing left to offer to society. That mentality needs to change. If you or anyone you know has had an experience with the incarceration of any sort, then you know how important it is to share this book with others. The only way we can reverse this troubling trend of mass incarceration is by rebutting societies and politicians' misconception about criminality. You can do a huge public service by spreading the news about it. You can make a difference. We cannot stand idly by as mass incarceration ruins people's lives. Take the message to everyone you know. Take it to people you don't know. Collectively, we can bring awareness to this issue.

About the Author

Daniel Jerimiah Simms has been ensnared in the criminal justice system since the age of thirteen due to bad choices, poverty, street life and a governmental system of oppression that incarcerates its American citizens rather than treating and training them in a career. Currently, Daniel is incarcerated with a thirty-two-year sentence for essentially a drug-deal robbery gone wrong. The cruelly long and harsh sentence has caused Daniel to fight vigorously to get his voice out to the world. Though the State of Washington has Daniel's body incarcerated, it does not have his mind imprisoned. If you would like to correspond or talk to Daniel you can do so at www.jpay.com.

www.ingramcontent.com/pod-product-compliance
Lightning Source LLC
Chambersburg PA
CBHW071900070526
44583CB00016B/1782